WISA
Wellness Improvement System
Assessment Instrument

Interpersonal Wellness Publishing, 2016.

www.interpersonalwellness.com

ISBN 978-0-9736067-6-8

Content

Congratulations!

You've just taken the first step toward creating a richer and fuller life that will increase your resilience and ability bounce back from life challenges.

What will it take to live your life well?

The WISA instrument will provide a wellness score for each of the eight wellness dimensions, an individual score for each of the five key life areas you measured, and one overall score that represents your WISA PROFILE, which is your wellness capacity.

Get ready to measure your wellness so you can better understand what it takes to stay well, and become empowered to better control and improve your wellness so you can excel.

A time to experience your best self

On pages 29 and 30 you gain information to help interpret your scores. In addition, you can also share your scores with your coach. At the end of completing this assessment, you may ask your facilitator to provide you with the more detailed WISA PROFILE report, which is a more comprehensive and tailored interpretation of your scores in each dimension. This can be used to help you develop a life wellness action plan.

Assessing Your Capacity
To Live Your Life Well

And be Resilient

Introduction

Welcome to the Wellness Revolution!

Step into a new dimension of wellness and explore some new concepts.

Everyday we are faced with challenges and stresses that erodes our wellness, weakening our resolve and making us vulnerable to overwhelm, stress and disease. The level of stress we now face is more than humans have been exposed in any age before our time.

If you've been wondering about being more resilient. This booklet will help you explore ways to build resilience so you can weather the storms and stresses of life.

Resilience requires you to strive for optimal wellness in all areas of life, thus you will be less vulnerable to breakdown. There is varying degrees to which any one dimension will contribute to our relationship wellness, but one's wellness in all of the eight dimensions can jointly determine their overall health and wellness, serving as a buffer to high stress and even crisis situations.

This wellness assessment instrument is designed to help you assess your WISA PROFILE™, which quantifies how well you are doing in each life dimension, to reveal your capacity to remain resilient in the face of life and relationship stresses. If you are curious about your capacity to be resilient, this exercise will help you see just how much wellness you have to contribute to the relationships in your life. The WISA PROFILE will help you measure, understand, control, and improve your life wellness in all areas, towards optimal wellness and resilience.

The instrument is designed to raise awareness and provoke additional questions, while exploring relevant areas and issues in your life. It will also provide a framework for understanding aspects of your life that may not be as satisfying as you would like.

Please note that this score is only a reflection of where things are in your life right now. If you don't like the results, you can take strategic steps to develop all eight wellness dimensions towards maximizing your business and personal success.

Wellness Improvement System Model

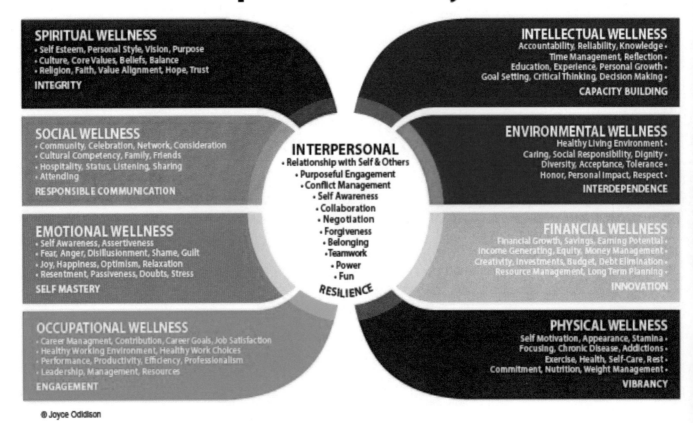

SPIRITUAL WELLNESS
- Self Esteem, Personal Style, Vision, Purpose
- Culture, Core Values, Beliefs, Balance
- Religion, Faith, Value Alignment, Hope, Trust

INTEGRITY

INTELLECTUAL WELLNESS
Accountability, Reliability, Knowledge -
Time Management, Reflection -
Education, Experience, Personal Growth -
Goal Setting, Critical Thinking, Decision Making -

CAPACITY BUILDING

SOCIAL WELLNESS
- Community, Celebration, Network, Consideration
- Cultural Competency, Family, Friends
- Hospitality, Status, Listening, Sharing
- Attending

RESPONSIBLE COMMUNICATION

ENVIRONMENTAL WELLNESS
Healthy Living Environment -
Caring, Social Responsibility, Dignity -
Diversity, Acceptance, Tolerance -
Honor, Personal Impact, Respect -

INTERDEPENDENCE

INTERPERSONAL
- Relationship with Self & Others
- Purposeful Engagement
- Conflict Management
    - Self Awareness
    - Collaboration
    - Negotiation
    - Forgiveness
    - Belonging
    - Teamwork
    - Power
    - Fun

RESILIENCE

EMOTIONAL WELLNESS
- Self Awareness, Assertiveness
- Fear, Anger, Disillusionment, Shame, Guilt
- Joy, Happiness, Optimism, Relaxation
- Resentment, Passiveness, Doubts, Stress

SELF MASTERY

FINANCIAL WELLNESS
Financial Growth, Savings, Earning Potential -
Income Generating, Equity, Money Management -
Creativity, Investments, Budget, Debt Elimination -
Resource Management, Long Term Planning -

INNOVATION

OCCUPATIONAL WELLNESS
- Career Managment, Contribution, Career Goals, Job Satisfaction
- Healthy Working Environment, Healthy Work Choices
- Performance, Productivity, Efficiency, Professionalism
- Leadership, Management, Resources

ENGAGEMENT

PHYSICAL WELLNESS
Self Motivation, Appearance, Stamina -
Focusing, Chronic Disease, Addictions -
Exercise, Health, Self-Care, Rest -
Commitment, Nutrition, Weight Management -

VIBRANCY

® Joyce Oddison

Learn Your Wellness Profile

Living purposefully in the **Spiritual, Social, Emotional, Occupational, Intellectual, Environmental, Financial** and **Physical** dimensions of your life is the key to great health and vitality. Gain insight and become equipped to transform your relationships, maximize your influence, creativity, contentment, prosperity and success. Learn how you are doing in all the dimensions above!

These dimensions make up your personal and interpersonal wellness system – how well you are, determines the level of wellness you can give to your relationships. The WELLNESS PROFILE will help you become aware of what is going on inside and outside of yourself and the relationship between the dimensions and how you experience your interpersonal relationships.

Instructions

Please score yourself by choosing any five key life areas from each dimension. Key life areas are different within each dimension as is outlined. Choose the key life areas that are relevant or important to you at this time in your life. Give yourself a score using numbers between 1 and 10, where 1= poor and 10 = excellent.

You can use any number between one and ten to rate how well you think you are doing in the five key life areas of your choice under each of the eight dimensions.

Ask yourself any of the following five questions to help rate yourself:

1. How well am I doing in this key life area?
2. How well am I feeling or experiencing this key life area?
3. How well are those in my life or business network experiencing me in this key life area?
4. Am I experiencing my optimal wellness in this key life area?
5. Do I want more for myself in this key life area?

You may **choose only five key life areas to assess in each dimension**, so choose the ones that are most relevant to your life **at this time**. These could be areas you are curious about, areas you want to develop, or areas you have never thought of before today.

As you go through the WIS assessment, you will need to make some decisions about who you are and how you want to experience certain areas of your life. This will determine how you feel about where things currently are in each area and will be reflected in the numeric score you assign to yourself. Please follow the instructions on the next page.

Please see example on the next page...

Sample Assessment

This person has picked the following five key life areas in the **Emotional Dimension** to assess his emotional wellness Profile. He has given himself a rating between one and ten for each of the key life areas that he has chosen by asking himself the five questions from the previous page.

1. How well I'm I doing in the area of self-esteem?
2. How well I'm I feeling or experiencing joy in my life?
3. How well are those in my life or work experiencing my expression of anger?
4. I'm I experiencing my optimal wellness in the way I express my doubts?
5. Do I want more for myself in the area of optimism?

Emotional Wellness Dimension Assessment

Emotional Wellness Dimension	Area Score
Self-awareness	7
Joy	8.5
Anger	8
Doubts	7
Optimism	9
	Total score = 39
	Total Score ÷ 5 = 7.9
	Emotional Wellness Profile = 7.9

Gain the knowledge you need to.....
Live Your Life Well

Let's Get Started!

Spiritual Wellness Dimension

A time to go inside self

Integrity

This dimension has a number of areas that are essential to living in integrity with your values. The wellness of your Spiritual Dimension will reflect how well you live in integrity and alignment with your values and how balances your life and defines your purpose. This will help you identify your wellness Profile in this dimension.

Pick any five key life areas of your choice from the list below to begin assessing your wellness in this dimension. Remember to ask yourself the five questions from page five, as per the example on page six, in order to rate yourself.

Key Life Areas

1. **Self-Esteem** – Having a sense of self-worth and self-value
2. **Personal Style** – Knowing your personal impact and energy field
3. **Culture** – Knowing the source of your beliefs and practices
4. **Core Values** – Knowing and holding firm to your values
5. **Belief** – Having confidence, deep conviction or certainty about something
6. **Religion** – Being affiliated to a church, denomination or religious group
7. **Faith** – Having confidence, trust and conviction in something or someone
8. **Integrity** – Being reliable, honest and trustworthy
9. **Balance** – Having steadiness of mind, convictions or temperance
10. **Hope** – Having an ability to trust or anticipate
11. **Vision** – Having an ability to dream, visualize or have great ideas
12. **Trust** – Being able to rely on others or being one that others can depend on

Score

Enter the five key life areas you have chosen on the previous page into the table below, assigning a score by choosing a number between one and ten that represents how well you are experiencing each key life area and how well others are experiencing you in this key life area.

Then complete the process by adding the five scores and divide the sum by five to arrive at your wellness Profile for this dimension.

Spiritual Dimension	Area Score
	Total Score =
	Total Score ÷ 5 =
	Spiritual Wellness Profile =

Social Wellness Dimension

SOCIAL
- Community, Celebration
- Family, Friends, Network
- Hospitality, Status
- Responsible Communication
- Cultural Competency

Responsible Communication

A time to build community

This dimension will reflect your ability to communicate responsibly in the various network of relationships in your life. The wellness of your Social Dimension will reflect how well you are able to communicate, negotiate and navigate through the various network cultures personal and professionally to harness the energy and opportunities they present. It will also determine your wellness in this dimension.

Pick any five key life areas of your choice from the list below to begin assessing your wellness in this dimension. Remember to ask yourself the five questions from page five, as per the example on page six, in order to help you rate yourself.

Key Life Areas

1. **Community** – Having a stable constituency of people, neighbourhood or group you belong to
2. **Status** – Having a position of importance, high regard or being popular in one's network
3. **Family** – Having great relationships with parents, children or spouse
4. **Friends** – Having a circle of caring, nurturing people you spend time with
5. **Responsible Communication** – Communicating with an intention to express care and concern for the relationship
6. **Cultural Competency** – Having the ability to negotiate the culture of your various relationships
7. **Network** – Interacting with a group of friends, family, co-workers and community of people with whom you associate and share your life
8. **Hospitality** – Being warm and welcoming to others
9. **Celebration** – Taking time to celebrate important milestones with loved ones

Score

Enter the five key life areas you have chosen on the previous page into the table below, assigning a score by choosing a number between one and ten that represents how well you are experiencing each key life area and how well others are experiencing you in this key life area.

Then complete the process by adding the five scores and divide the sum by five to arrive at your wellness Profile for this dimension.

Social Dimension	Area Score
	Total Score =
	Total Score ÷ 5 =
	Social Wellness Profile =

Emotional Wellness Dimension

A time to manage self

Self-Mastery

This dimension has a number of key life areas that are essential to developing self-mastery. The wellness of your Emotional Dimension will reflect how well you are able to harness the energy in the network of relationships in your life, as well as negotiate and embrace their various cultures. It will also help you identify your wellness Profile in this dimension.

Pick any five key life areas of your choice from the list below to begin assessing your wellness in this dimension. Remember to ask yourself the five questions from page five, as per the example on page six, in order to help you rate yourself.

Key Life Areas

1. **Self-Awareness** – Being aware of yourself and your impact on others
2. **Assertiveness** – Being able to communicate clearly and directly in order to have needs met
3. **Fear** – Having unnecessary feelings of panic, fright, dread or terror
4. **Anger** – Being able to manage feelings of anger well and responsibly
5. **Disillusionment** – Having cynicism, disappointment, dissatisfaction and displeasure
6. **Joy** – Experiencing happiness, delight or pleasure
7. **Shame** – Strong feelings of embarrassment, humiliation, disgrace or dishonor
8. **Happiness** – Being content, pleased and glad with life and self
9. **Guilt** – blaming self, feelings of culpability, self-incrimination
10. **Optimism** – Being hopeful, positive, confident and cheerful
11. **Resentment** – Having feelings of bitterness, dislike, hatred and offensiveness
12. **Passiveness** – Being docile, meek, quiet, unassuming, submissive, dutiful
13. **Doubts** – Having feelings of worry, misgiving, uncertainty and reservation
14. **Stress** – Having feelings of strain, pressure, heaviness, responsibility
15. **Relaxation** – Making time for leisure, recreation, meditation, respite from stress and worry

Score

Enter the five key life areas you have chosen on the previous page into the table below, assigning a score by choosing a number between one and ten that represents how well you are experiencing each key life area and how well others are experiencing you in this key life area.

Then complete the process by adding the five scores and divide the sum by five to arrive at your wellness Profile for this dimension.

Note: *for key life areas such as anger or resentment, one who has a lot of anger or resentment will rate between one and three, since a lot of anger is not good for one's wellness.*

Emotional Dimension	Area Score
	Total Score =
	Total Score ÷ 5 =
	Emotional Wellness Profile =

Occupational Wellness Dimension

OCCUPATIONAL
- Job Skills, Position, Career Goals
- Healthy Work Environment
- Job training level, Job Performance
- Job Satisfaction, Career Opportunity
- Competencies, Problem Solving

A time for achievement

Engagement

This dimension has a number of key life areas that are essential to you making a meaningful commitment and engaging with your career or life work. The wellness of your Occupational Dimension will reflect how well you are able to engage and commit to something you enjoy. It will also help you identify your wellness Profile in this dimension.

Pick any five key life areas of your choice from the list below to begin assessing your wellness in this dimension. Remember to ask yourself the five questions from page five, as per the example on page six, in order to help you rate yourself.

Key Life Areas

1. **Job Skills** – Achieving an appropriate level of job expertise, dexterity, talent or proficiency
2. **Job Position** – Holding a job in a position that is rewarding, well situated, appealing
3. **Career Goals** – Having clear career goals to advance or accelerate one's career
4. **Job Performance** – Performing job well, displaying great work ethics, ability to perform necessary tasks
5. **Healthy Work Environment** – Contributing to work environment with good working relationships, collaboration and opportunity to participate in decision-making
6. **Job Satisfaction** – Being content, pleased and fulfilled by job
7. **Competencies** – Having proficiency and aptitude, capability and know-how necessary for job
8. **Problem Solving** – Having the ability to cope with job challenges and address difficulties
9. **Supervision** – Being aware of the rules and having support to manage workload
10. **Leadership** – Having clear directions and understanding of the way forward
11. **Performance** – Demonstrating a consistent effort towards required level of work

Score

Enter the five key life areas you have chosen on the previous page into the table below, assigning a score by choosing a number between one and ten that represents how well you are experiencing each key life area and how well others are experiencing you in this key life area.

Then complete the process by adding the five scores and divide the sum by five to arrive at your wellness Profile for this dimension.

Occupational Dimension	Area Score
	Total Score =
	Total Score ÷ 5 =
	Occupational Wellness Profile =

Intellectual Wellness Dimension

INTELLECTUAL
Accountability, Reliability, Knowledge •
Time Management, Problem Solving, •
Education, Experience, Personal Growth •
Ability to set Goals, Good Decision Making •
Reflection, Critical Thinking, Risk Taking •

Capacity Building

A time for growth

This dimension has a number of key life areas that are essential for capacity building. The wellness of your Intellectual Dimension will reflect your capacity for growth and development. It will also help you identify your wellness Profile in this dimension.

Pick any five key life areas of your choice from the list below to begin assessing your wellness in this dimension. Remember to ask yourself the five questions from page five, as per the example on page six, in order to help you rate yourself.

Key Life Areas

1. **Accountability** – Being responsible or answerable for your actions
2. **Reliability** – Being dependable, reliable and consistent
3. **Knowledge** – Having knowledge of the things that matter to your life or work
4. **Education** – Having adequate learning for the life you desire to live?
5. **Experience** – Having past accumulated information, familiarity based on past, strength
6. **Personal Growth** – Taking action to learn and develop a deeper awareness of self
7. **Problem Solving** – Having the ability to decipher, unravel, work things out and form solutions
8. **Decision-Making** – Showing good judgment and making choices that are good for ones well-being
9. **Time Management** – Using time well, ability to organize, prioritize and schedule
10. **Goal Setting** – Setting attainable goals, having an aim, objective and purpose for ones actions
11. **Reflection** – Being contemplative, to mull over and be introspective about things
12. **Critical Thinking** – Being able to see what's vital or missing, to think outside the box, make good assessments

Score

Enter the five key life areas you have chosen on the previous page into the table below, assigning a score by choosing a number between one and ten that represents how well you are experiencing each key life area and how well others are experiencing you in this key life area.

Then complete the process by adding the five scores and divide the sum by five to arrive at your wellness Profile for this dimension.

Intellectual Dimension	Area Score
	Total Score =
	Total Score ÷ 5 =
	Intellectual Wellness Profile =

Environmental Wellness Dimension

ENVIRONMENTAL
Personal Impact •
Social Consciousness •
Diversity, Acceptance, Tolerance •
Interdependence, Respect •
Healthy Living Environment•

Interdependence

This dimension has a number of key life areas that are essential to your interdependence. Remember that the wellness of your Environmental Dimension will reflect your capacity to live in harmony with others and with the universe. We each have a social responsibility to give more than we take and a moral obligation to respect others and treat them with dignity. It will also help you identify your wellness Profile in this dimension.

Pick any five key life areas of your choice from the list below to begin assessing your wellness in this dimension. Remember to ask yourself the five questions from page five, as per the example on page six, in order to help you rate yourself.

Key Life Areas

1. **Diversity** – Being able to accept differences in others and in self
2. **Social Consciousness** – Having awareness and acknowledging one's responsibility to others and the universe, caring for the wellbeing of others, the community and environment
3. **Personal Impact** – Being aware of how your behaviour affects or irritates others
4. **Healthy Living Environment** – Taking care of your living or work area, ensuring safety by cleaning up after oneself and caring for your surroundings
5. **Acceptance** – Receiving and approving of others with kindness, without judgement
6. **Tolerance** – Being broad-minded, open minded and understanding of other's preferences
7. **Social Responsibility** – Giving back to society and community, protecting the environment or where one lives or works
8. **Interdependence** – Having shared dependence, being interconnected and realizing one's need of others
9. **Respect** – Treating others with dignity, valuing others, self-esteem, having reverence for nature

Score

Enter the five key life areas you have chosen on the previous page into the table below, assigning a score by choosing a number between one and ten that represents how well you are experiencing each key life area and how well others are experiencing you in this key life area.

Then complete the process by adding the five scores and divide the sum by five to arrive at your wellness Profile for this dimension.

Environmental Dimension	Area Score
	Total Score =
	Total Score ÷ 5 =
	Environmental Wellness Profile =

Financial Wellness Dimension

FINANCIAL
Earning Potential •
Money Management •
Budget, Debt Load •
Long Term Planning •
Equity, Investments, Savings •

Innovation

This dimension has a number of key life areas that are essential to our ability to be innovative. The wellness of your Financial Dimension will reflect your capacity to plan for the long-term, think expansively and to budget your time and resources to build equity. It will also help you identify your wellness Profile in this dimension.

Pick any five key life areas of your choice from the list below to begin assessing your wellness in this dimension. Remember to ask yourself the five questions from page five, as per the example on page six, in order to help you rate yourself.

Key Life Areas

1. **Earning Potential** – Having capacity to increase one's income, resources or net worth
2. **Money Management** – Being skilled at using money wisely and making sound decisions about money
3. **Debt Load** – Being aware of one's debt capacity and being wise to not exceed comfortable debt
4. **Budget** – Having a plan to account for one's money, time and resources
5. **Long Term Planning** – Planning and forecasting for the long-term
6. **Equity** – Accumulating money, time and resources
7. **Savings** – Having a reserve or nest egg of money or resources that has been put aside
8. **Investment** – Having an earning or return on money, property, resources that is growing

Score

Enter the five key life areas you have chosen on the previous page into the table below, assigning a score by choosing a number between one and ten that represents how well you are experiencing each key life area and how well others are experiencing you in this key life area.

Then complete the process by adding the five scores and divide the sum by five to arrive at your wellness Profile for this dimension.

Financial Dimension	Area Score
	Total Score =
	Total Score ÷ 5 =
	Financial Wellness Profile =

Physical Wellness Dimension

PHYSICAL
Appearance, Stamina •
Chronic Disease, Addictions •
Exercise, Health, Self-Care, Rest •
Nutrition, Weight Management •
Focusing, Self Motivation •

Vibrancy

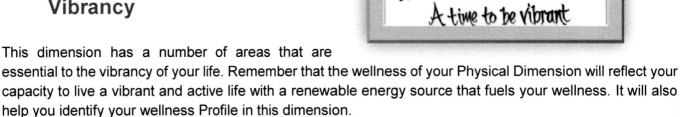

A time to be vibrant

This dimension has a number of areas that are essential to the vibrancy of your life. Remember that the wellness of your Physical Dimension will reflect your capacity to live a vibrant and active life with a renewable energy source that fuels your wellness. It will also help you identify your wellness Profile in this dimension.

Please pick any five key life areas of your choice from the list below to begin assessing your wellness in this dimension. Remember to ask yourself the five questions from page five, as per the example on page six, in order to help you rate yourself.

Key Life Areas

1. **Appearance** – Presenting a positive, healthy outward appearance, look or image
2. **Stamina** – Having endurance, staying power, resilience and energy
3. **Exercise** – Moving one's body and being active or physical
4. **Health** – Being in a state of good physical health, vigour, wellbeing, without disease
5. **Self-Care** – Caring for self, keeping clean, groomed, well fed, active and rested
6. **Rest** – Relaxing, getting enough sleep, taking breaks and observing down time
7. **Nutrition** – Maintaining a healthy, balanced diet with fruits, vegetables, protein and water
8. **Focusing** – Making physical wellness a priority
9. **Self-Motivation** – Being enthusiastic, inspired and driven to stay healthy
10. **Chronic Disease** – Having a disease, illness, syndrome or ailment that is uncontrolled
11. **Addictions** – Having a compulsion, need, craving to use a substance in excess such as alcohol, illicit drugs, tobacco, food or other harmful practices

Score

Enter the five key life areas you have chosen on the previous page into the table below, assigning a score by choosing a number between one and ten that represents how well you are experiencing each key life area and how well others are experiencing you in this key life area.

Then complete the process by adding the five scores and divide the sum by five to arrive at your wellness Profile for this dimension.

Physical Dimension	Area Score
	Total Score =
	Total Score ÷ 5 =
	Physical Wellness Profile =

Completing Your WISA PROFILE

Now that you have completed your wellness assessment, you will have a total of eight wellness Profiles, one for each wellness dimension. Please transfer each to the table below and add your scores together, then divide the total by eight to get your WISA PROFILE. This will be used to generate your WISA Profile Report and aid you in developing a more personalized Wellness Life Plan.

Let's Get Started!

Transfer your wellness Profile scores for each dimension below, total all eight scores and divide the sum by eight to get your WISA PROFILE.

Spiritual	Social	Emotional	Occupational	Intellectual	Environmental	Financial	Physical
Total =	Total =	Total =	Total =	Total =	Total =	Total =	Total =
Total Score =							

Total of all 8 scores = _____ ÷ 8 = _____ **WISA PROFILE**

Congratulations!

You have successfully completed the WISA Instrument, which will help us generate your wellness life plan

You are now ready to work with your facilitator or coach to identify your wellness profile and review the corresponding wellness level. This report will give you some further interpretation of your scores and help you in executing your Life Plan to attain optimal wellness in all eight wellness dimensions.

You can choose to complete the next exercise, which is an interpersonal audit of a relationship of your choice.

Interpersonal Relationship Audit

INTERPERSONAL
- Relationship with Self & Others
- Conflict Management
- Positive Vibrations
- Self Awareness
- Collaboration
- Belonging
- Esteem
- Power
- Fun

A time to experience your best self

Purposeful Engagement

Now that you have completed a WISA profile, the following exercise will provide you with an interpersonal assessment of a relationship of your choice below:

1. __ Parent/Guardian
2. __ Sibling/Child
3. __ Supervisor/Manager/Team Leader
4. __ Spouse/Partner
5. __ Neighbour/Community/Church

Please answer the following questions about your relationship, using the same scale of 1 – 10, 1 being poor and 10 being excellent, to measure the level of wellness in your relationship.

1. Rate the level of understanding of yourself and the other party in this relationship____
2. Rate your ability to manage conflict in this relationship ____
3. Rate the level of positive social vibrations created in this relationship____
4. Rate the level of self-motivating power you draw from this relationship ____
5. Rate your level of support, assistance, team-work and collaboration that you give in this relationship____
6. Rate the level of support, assistance, team-work and collaboration that you receive in this relationship ____

7. Rate how well you fit-in or your sense of belonging in this relationship _____

8. Rate how you regard and admire the other party in this relationship _____

9. Rate how well the other party regards and admires you_____

10. Rate your level of influence in this relationship _____

11. Rate the level of influence that the other party in this relationship has on you _____

12. Rate the level of fun you have in this relationship _____

Interpersonal Audit Questions	Score
1.	
2.	
3.	
4.	
5.	
6.	
7.	
8.	
9.	
10.	
11.	
12.	
	Total = _____ ÷ 12
	Total Score =

Congratulations! You have completed your assessment.

Interpreting Your Score

In each wellness dimension, you have received a Profile that ranges between one and ten. Your score range signifies your wellness level and profile. Below is an interpretation of both your current wellness level and its profile. You can use this interpretation to help you plan the next steps for improving your wellness in any one dimension or your overall WISA PROFILE.

You can attain wellness levels between one and eight in each dimension. Level eight represents the optimal and is the highest level of wellness. The assumption is that Wellness Level 8 will be different for you at each stage of your life.

Wellness Dimension Profile Score Range – Wellness Level	Wellness Profile - Interpretation
Wellness Level 8 Score Range: 9 – 10	**Optimal Wellness** –You are at your optimal wellness in this wellness dimension for the areas you have assessed. You are receiving great energy and sustenance from this dimension that is impacting your vitality. You are ready to experience the next stage of business and life success. **Congratulations!** Take some time to celebrate.
Wellness Level 7 Score Range: 8 – 9	**Success Wellness** –You are experiencing high wellness success. Your energy flow is impacting others as positive social vibrations. As a result, you are experiencing others well, but have identified an area or two where you would like to improve. Don't ever stop growing and learning, it is why you were created.
Wellness Level 6 Score Range: 7 – 8	**Achieved Wellness** – You worked hard and have achieved great wellness in your life. You are however hampered by a few key life areas that you have left unaddressed. It is time to refocus and begin taking care of all areas of your life in order to achieve your optimal wellness.
Wellness Level 5 Score Range: 6 – 7	**Moderate Wellness** – You are experiencing good wellness, but it is not at your optimal range. You should acknowledge yourself for having such positive intentions. Now that you are aware, it is time to address those key life areas that are not working for you. Begin by being grateful for what you have and open yourself to the new realities that you can create in your life.

Wellness Level 4 Score Range: 5 – 6	**Borderline Wellness** – You are neither doing great nor poorly, but leaving your wellness at this range can have a harmful impact and lead to you becoming unwell. Take some time to think of the things in your life that you are grateful for and begin by listing two reasons to improve your wellness in the next three months to help motivate you in your wellness development.
Wellness Level 3 Score Range: 4 – 5	**Diminishing Wellness** – You are beginning to lose control of your wellness. It is time to make a list of things in your life you can change and identify one or two things you can do that will enhance how you experience your life.
Wellness Level 2 Score Range: 3 – 4	**Disrupted Wellness** – Your energy field has been disrupted. You spend most of your time focusing on things outside yourself and taking very little time to consider how you want to experience others or have them experience their interactions with you. It's time to look at yourself and begin working on your wellness.
Wellness Level 1 Score Range: 1 – 3	**Wellness Deficit** – Your energy flow is distorted and having a negative impact on your overall wellness. You are now in a wellness deficit, which is accounting for you being overwhelmed and unmotivated. As a result, you are unaware of your impact on others and you are responding in a manner that is being viewed as reactive, suspicious and defensive.
Total WELLNESS PROFILE	

Now that you have completed the WISA instrument, you should obtain your full Wellness Profile Report. You can do so in any of the following ways:

- Contact your Wellness Facilitator or
- Contact your Wellness Coach or
- Go online to interpersonalwellness.com or
- Call 204 668-5283 and ask for the link to the WISA report.

Congratulations!

WISA
Life Plan Profile

Get ready to create your WLP

Enter your WISA level and profile score in the first two columns and set the wellness goal you would like to attain in the far right column.

Ask yourself the following questions:

1. Where would you like to improve your wellness capacity?

2. What is your intention for your wellness in these key life areas in the next six months?

Wellness Dimension	Wellness Level	Wellness Profile	Wellness Goal
Spiritual Dimension			
Social Dimension			
Emotional Dimension			
Occupational Dimension			
Intellectual Dimension			
Environmental Dimension			
Financial Dimension			
Physical Dimension			

Ask your facilitator or coach to help you develop a wellness life plan (WLP). You can develop a more elaborate action plan to optimize your WISA PROFILE in the next few months.

Access the electronic WISA assessment, should you choose to complete it online at www.wellnessassessment.ca

Wellness Builds Resiliency

Own your Wellness!

Though access to personal training and coaching is better than ever, more professionals are facing burnout and overwhelm. The need to stay abreast of so much information and lending yourself to various projects is taxing. Without appropriate help, professionals will continue to encounter interpersonal conflict, health problems and even premature death for some leaders.

The need to improve resilience for leaders is greater than ever before, to sustain them through the stresses of their business, careers and lives. Since 2012, WISA has given leaders an opportunity to step back and put things in perspective, by creating awareness so they can pay attention to where they may be leaking vital energy, to make necessary changes.

WISA has helped leaders create a roadmap to whole life wellness and prepare themselves better to withstand the assault of work and life stress better. Working with WISA have allowed leaders to build resilience to withstand professional and personal stresses better.

What intentions do you hold for your relationships?

About Us

We are a performance enhancement consulting, coaching and training firm that provides strategic solutions to reduce interpersonal conflicts, and enhance employee performance, teamwork, productivity, efficiency and workplace wellness.

We provide Interpersonal Wellness audits, executive coaching, conflict management, wellness, and respectful workplace interventions, and a fully certified coach training program.

Our services have been proven to help client organizations improve efficiency, collaboration and workplace wellness.

We are committed to bringing you world class innovations to improve performance and employee engagement and wellness. We use tools such as the Wellness Improvement System®, WISA Instrument, the Wellness Life Plan and the Wellness for Business and Life® coaching programs and retreats.

We develop capacity within organizations with our Interpersonal Wellness Coaching and Wellness Facilitator Training and Licence programs.

We welcome your thoughts and feedback on the WISA Personal Assessment Instrument.

Tell us your stories and successes; let us know how you are using this tool to help revolutionize the wellness of your workplaces and teams.

To learn more or to contact us, go to www.interpersonalwellness.com

WISA Personal Instrument

Order Form

Name: _____

Company: _____

Address: _____

City/Province: _____

Tel: _____ Fax: _____

E-Mail: _____

Cost of Book: $15.00 each plus 5% GST

Please add $4.00 for shipping and handling in Canada, and $8.00 for orders outside Canada.

Total # of books ____

Order by fax, phone or e-mail: admin@interpersonalwellness.com

Make cheques payable to Interpersonal Wellness Services Inc.

Method of Payment ___ Cheque ___ Invoice ___ Visa ___ Master Card

Credit Card #: _____ Expiry Date _____

Signature: _____

Interpersonal Wellness Services Inc.
845 Henderson Hwy., Winnipeg, MB R2K 2L4
Phone: 204 668-5283
Fax: 204 667-8845
Toll Free 1 877 999-9591
Website: www.interpersonalwellness.com

Made in the USA
Lexington, KY
22 August 2019